A Tree Lives

Written by
Richard Lewis
Illustrated by
Noah Baen

With additional art and writing by children
from the East Village Community School,
New York City

Designed by
Heidi Neilson
Photographed by
George Hirose

Touchstone Center Publications

*To Robin Ross, who helps my roots grow deep
and my leaves open to the light.*
—N. B.

*To my grandchildren, Benjamin and Daniel:
May you always know yourselves—and the world—by climbing trees.*
—R. L.

Library of Congress Control Number: 2005900339
ISBN: 1-929299-04-4

Touchstone Center Publications
141 East 88th Street
New York, NY 10128
Tel: 212-831-7717
Fax: 212-427-9644
rlewis212@aol.com
www.touchstonecenter.net

To the Reader

A tree knows when to let its leaves open. It knows how to take water from its roots, how to bend with the wind, how to grow tall and full and alive.

A tree even knows when to sleep, letting its leaves fall to the ground, its branches waiting for another spring.

But does a tree know the wetness of rain, the cold of winter snow? Does it know how dark the night becomes, how long a day can be?

Can it smell the air?
Can it hear the birds?
Can it see the sky?

Because a tree is, can it ask, can it answer?

Can it, like us, imagine?

In our backyard,
a tree lives.

In its leaves—

spring winds.

In its branches—
hungry birds.

In its roots—

moving waters.

And inside this tree

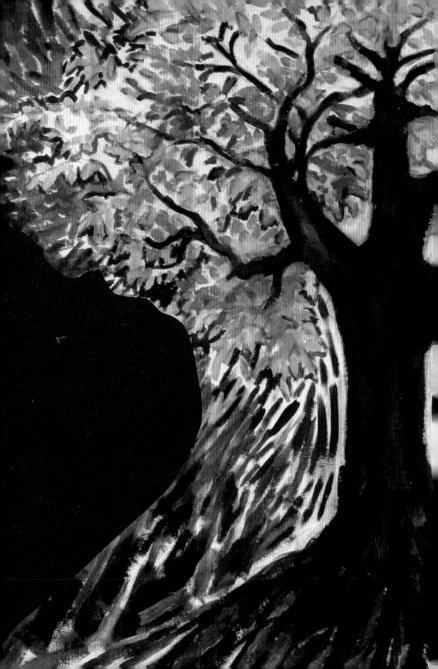

another tree
lives.

In its leaves—

distant skies.

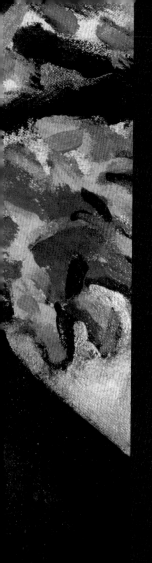

In its branches—
shadows of stars.

In its roots—

dreaming darkness.

And further inside

another tree lives.

In its leaves—

a moon grows.

In its branches—
the sun returns.

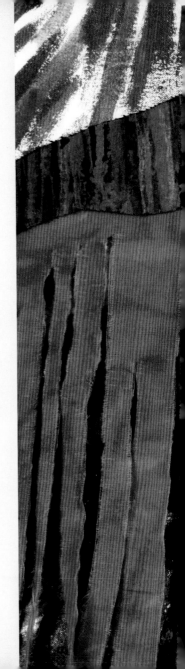

In its roots—
a day begins.

And further still

is there
another tree—

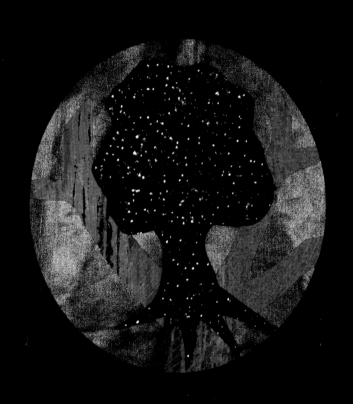

another tree
living inside?

The Tree of Knowing Project

Before becoming the illustrations for this book, Noah Baen's artwork was a large unfolding sculptural painting created as the centerpiece for a theatre work based on the present text of *A Tree Lives*. With music by Harry Mann, *A Tree Lives* was first performed in February 2003 as the starting point of a ten-week series of one-hour workshops, part of a Touchstone Center arts and education residency entitled the Tree of Knowing Project. This two-year project, under the direction of Richard Lewis and Claudia Keel, took place at the East Village Community School, a public elementary school in New York City, in collaboration with the school's art teacher, Julie Kirkpatrick. The Tree of Knowing Project explored with two separate classrooms of children from the first through the sixth grades the unique and often hidden ways of knowing found in the life of a tree.

Following the performance of *A Tree Lives*, children were asked to create an oil pastel drawing of what they imagined to be their own 'tree of knowing'. In subsequent workshops this drawing evolved into a 20" x 40" acrylic painting on canvas by each child. In many instances these drawings and paintings become springboards for ongoing discussions and writing by the children. For the second year of the project, children were encouraged to envision the leaves and roots of their tree of knowing. These discoveries culminated in a final sharing of writings and paintings that are now displayed throughout the school. Both the children's work and the various images from Noah Baen's original sculptural painting were photographed by George Hirose, and then designed into a book by Heidi Neilson.

The artwork and writing that follow are examples of work by some of the children who participated in the Tree of Knowing Project as they brought their own imaginative understandings of the profound 'knowledge' that is nature into a new and vibrant reality.

I think the trees have a conversation of nature.
                                    —Qweshon, age 8

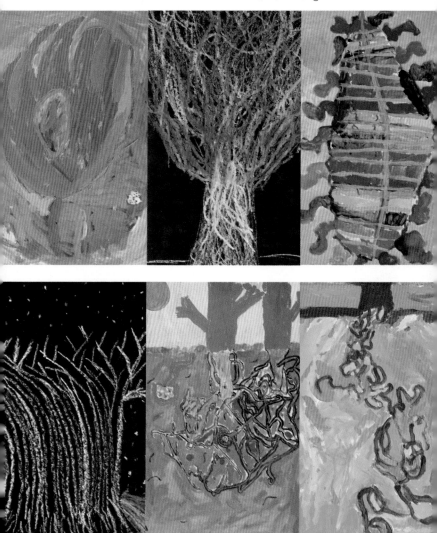

My tree likes to look at the stars and its leaves make the wind change colors.
My tree likes to give life to dead things.
                                    —Angie, age 10

My leaf needs kindness and stars and snow in order to grow.
—Valentine, age 7

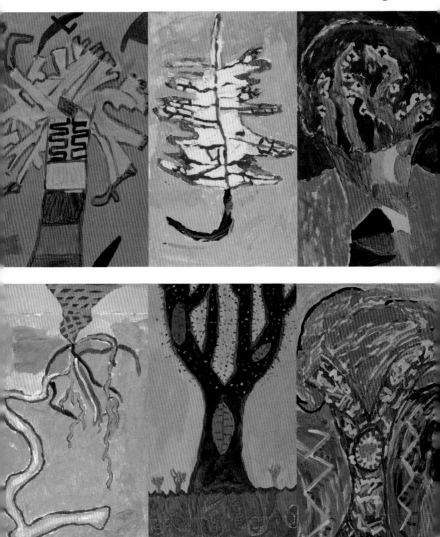

My tree knows that it's surrounded by wind.
My tree feels happy because it knows it's sparkling.
—Kevin, age 8

I think we know what a tree dreams—because at night we sleep next to a tree and it is like two thoughts together.

—Case, age 8

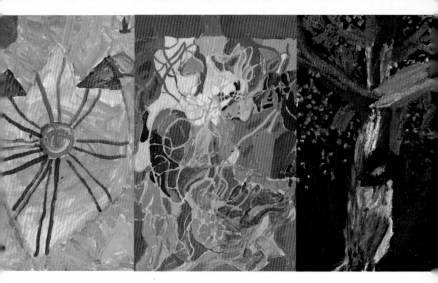

My roots have a heart, a heart that's the source of the tree.
My root's heart is like water that makes the tree live.

—Donovin, age 11

Acknowledgements

Our many thanks to all the children, teachers, staff, and parents at the East Village Community School who, with their genuine enthusiasm and inspiration, made the Tree of Knowing Project such a pleasure for us all. And to those children whose work we have the honor of reproducing in this book: Josh Asmall-Liversidge (age 11), Case Bongirne (age 8), Angie Bowkett (age 10), Qweshon Brown (age 8), Donovin Cabrera (age 11), Carriola Chambers (age 11), Tyrik Coleman (age 11), Jenise Colon (age 7), Kevin De la Cruz (age 8), LaPorsche Ellison (age 11), Kalinda Kelley (age 11), Tristan Lee (age 7), Natalie Mattson (age 7), Brittany Muñoz (age 7), Nadia Ogbor (age 11), Brooklyn Penson (age 11), Valentine Petrillo (age 7), Kenny Serano (age 8), Ned Steves (age 8), Rita Tuitt (age 8), and Sasha Wheeler (age 10).

Our special gratitude to Julie Kirkpatrick, for her sensitive and wise teaching; to Claudia Keel, for her gift of ripening children's artistic abilities; to Harry Mann, for his gentle music; to Lisa Bianco, Director of the East Village Community School, for her vision of learning; and to the classroom teachers Chaiti Sen, Rosemary Yim, and Roberta Valentine for their commitment and support throughout our residency.

And for the making of this book, my appreciation to Noah Baen, for his patience and the marvel of his imagery; to Heidi Neilson, for her luminous and original design work; to Kim Fisher, for his editorial insights; and to George Hirose, for the clarity of his seeing. And to my family for the constancy of their delight and love.

The Tree of Knowing Project was made possible by the generous support of the New York State Council on the Arts, the Project Arts Funds of the New York City Department of Education, the Parents Association of the East Village Community School, and the School Arts Rescue Initiative.

The Touchstone Center

is a nonprofit educational organization based in New York City. Since its founding in 1969, the Center has created, through its workshops, exhibitions, theatre productions, publications, and interdisciplinary arts programs in public schools a variety of ways to explore and sustain the importance of imaginative and poetic processes in all areas of learning.

Touchstone Center Publications

is a direct outgrowth of the Center's activities, and publishes and distributes publications that document the texts, themes, and images that have been instrumental in helping both children and adults express their innate imaginative relationships to the natural world.

The most recent publications of the Center include three titles, each of which has been made into an interpretive video by Geoffrey Jones and a traveling exhibit.

Each Sky Has Its Words, by Richard Lewis
Illustrated by Gigi Alvaré
ISBN: 1-929299-00-1

The Bird of Imagining, by Richard Lewis
Illustrated by children from New York City public schools
ISBN 1-929299-01-X

CAVE: An Evocation of the Beginnings of Art, by Richard Lewis
Sculpture by Elizabeth Crawford, photographed by George Hirose
ISBN 1-9299299-03-6

A Tree Lives

In our backyard, a tree lives.

In its leaves—spring winds.
In its branches—hungry birds.
In its roots—moving waters.

And inside this tree
another tree lives.

In its leaves—distant skies.
In its branches—shadows of stars.
In its roots—dreaming darkness.

And further inside
another tree lives.

In its leaves—a moon grows.
In its branches—the sun returns.
In its roots—a day begins.

And further still
is there another tree—

another tree
living inside?